Writing on Metal Plates

At times, even Book of Mormon
prophets got it wrong
(at first)

Compiled by
Philip M. Hudson

ISBN 978-1-950647-41-5

Illustrations – Google Images.

This book may be ordered from online bookstores.

Publishing Services by BookCrafters
Parker, Colorado.
www.bookcrafters.net

Table of Contents

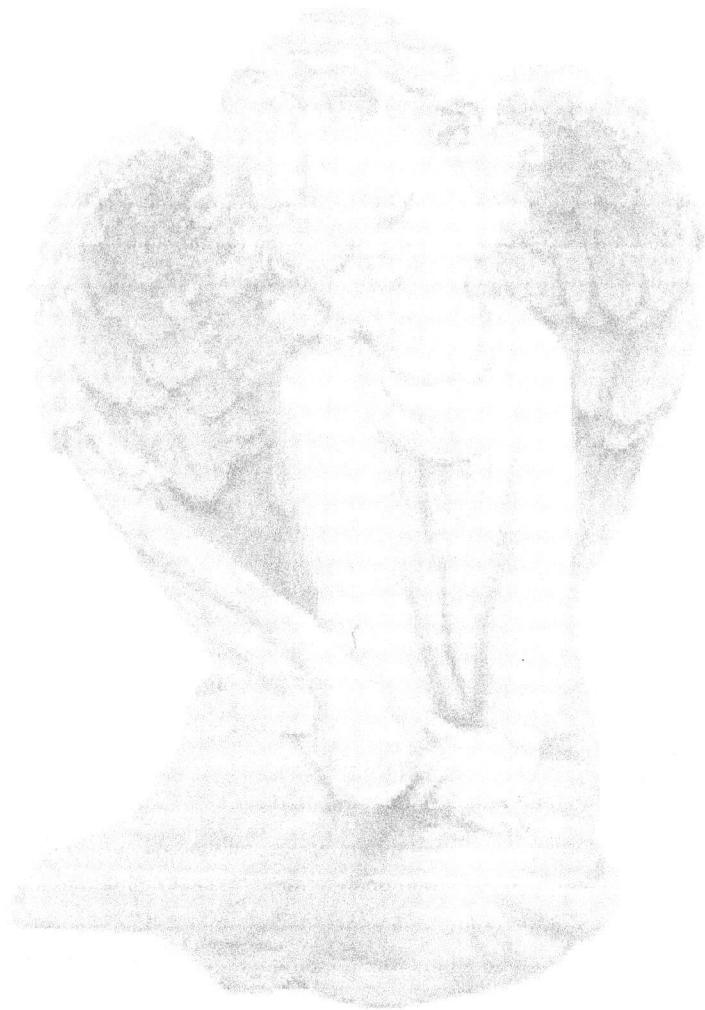

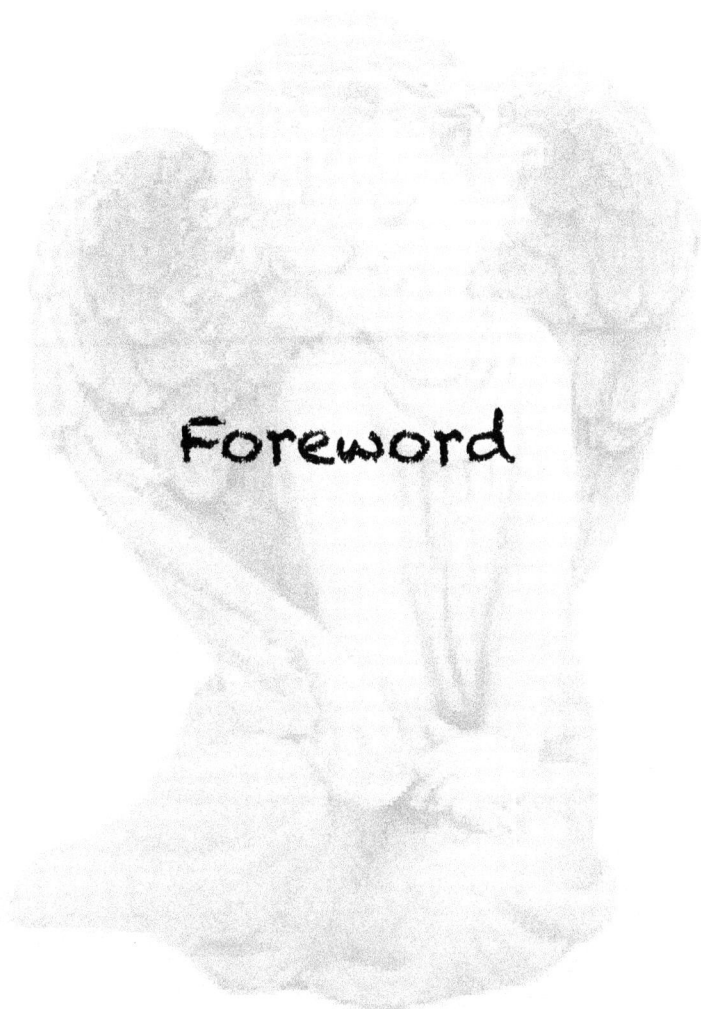

Foreword

Many passages
in The Book of Mormon
illustrate the difficulty of
engraving upon metal plates, and
of correcting that which had already
been written thereon. Nephi, Jacob, Alma,
Mormon, and Moroni, realizing that they
had not expressed themselves as they
had intended, added dozens of
of illuminating clarifications
that are sprinkled here and
there throughout
the text.

Mormon acknowledged his inability to communicate in writing as fluidly as he would have liked, by saying of the sacred records: "And if there be faults, they be the faults of a man." (Mormon 8:17).

Scriptures & Citations
in Chronological Order

2

"This
is according
to the account of
Nephi; or, in other words,
I, Nephi, wrote this record."
(Superscript to 1 Nephi 1).

4

"And it came to pass
that while my father tarried in
the wilderness he spake unto us
saying: Behold, I have dreamed
a dream, or, in other words,
I have seen a vision."
(1 Nephi 8:2).

6

"Yea, even six hundred years
from the time that my father left
Jerusalem, a prophet would the Lord
God raise up among the Jews — even
a Messiah, or, in other words,
a Savior of the world."
(1 Nephi 10:4).

8

"And that
great pit, which hath been
digged for them by that great
and abominable church, which was
founded by the devil and his children,
that he might lead away the souls of men
down to hell — yea, that great pit which hath
been digged for the destruction of men shall be
filled by those who digged it, unto their utter
destruction, saith the Lamb of God; not
the destruction of the soul, save it
be the casting of it into that
hell which hath no end."
(1 Nephi 14:3).

"They are
written in the book which
thou beheld proceeding out
of the mouth of the Jew; and at
the time they proceeded out of the
mouth of the Jew, or, at the time the
book proceeded out of the mouth
of the Jew, the things which were
written were plain and pure, and
most precious and easy to the
understanding of all men."
(1 Nephi 14:23).

"I do
not write anything
upon plates save it be that
I think it be sacred. And now,
if I do err, even did they err of
old; not that I would excuse myself
because of other men, but because
of the weakness which is in me,
according to the flesh, I
would excuse myself."
(1 Nephi 19:6).

14

"The very
God of Israel do men
trample under their feet; I say,
trample under their feet but I
would speak in other words
— they set him at naught,
and hearken not to the
voice of his counsels."
(1 Nephi 19:7).

"Hearken and hear
this, O house of Jacob,
who are called by the name
of Israel, and are come forth
out of the waters of Judah, or out
of the waters of baptism, who swear
by the name of the Lord, and make
mention of the God of Israel,
yet they swear not in truth
nor in righteousness."
(1 Nephi 20:1).

"Men are instructed sufficiently that they know good from evil. And the law is given unto men. And by the law no flesh is justified; or, by the law men are cut off. Yea, by the temporal law they were cut off; and also, by the spiritual law they perish from that which is good, and become miserable forever. Wherefore, redemption cometh in and through the Holy Messiah." (2 Nephi 2:5-6).

20

"I know that ye
have searched much,
many of you, to know
of things to come; wherefore
I know that ye know that our
flesh must waste away and die;
nevertheless, in our bodies
we shall see God."
(2 Nephi 9:4).

"I have
charity for the Jew; I
say Jew, because I mean
them from whence I came."
(2 Nephi 33:8).

"I, Jacob,
having ministered
much unto my people in
word, and I cannot write but a
little of my words, because of the
difficulty of engraving our words
upon plates, and we know that
the things which we write upon
plates must remain."
(Jacob 4:1).

"For this intent
have we written these things,
that they may know that we knew
of Christ, and we had a hope of his
glory many hundred years before his
coming; and not only we ourselves
had a hope of his glory, but also
all the holy prophets which were
before us." (Jacob 4:4).

"My beloved brethren, I will unfold this mystery unto you; if I do not, by any means, get shaken from my firmness in the Spirit, and stumble because of my over anxiety for you."
(Jacob 4:18).

"Salvation might
come to him that should put
his trust in the Lord, and should be
diligent in keeping his commandments,
and continue in the faith even unto
the end of his life, I mean the
life of the mortal body."
(Mosiah 4:6).

"And ye will not
suffer your children that they
go hungry, or naked; neither will
ye suffer that they transgress the laws
of God, and fight and quarrel one with
another, and serve the devil, who is the
master of sin, or who is the evil spirit
which hath been spoken of by our
fathers, he being an enemy
to all righteousness."
(Mosiah 4:14).

34

"I say unto the poor,
ye who have not and yet
have sufficient, that ye remain
from day to day; I mean all
you who deny the beggar,
because ye have not.
(Mosiah 4:24).

"We
believe all
the words which
thou hast spoken
unto us; and also, we
know of their surety and
truth, because of the Spirit
of the Lord Omnipotent, which
has wrought a mighty change in
us, or in our hearts, that we
have no more disposition
to do evil, but to do
good continually."
(Mosiah 5:2).

"He was
desirous to know
concerning the people who
went up to dwell in the land
of Lehi-Nephi, or in the
city of Lehi-Nephi."
(Mosiah 7:1).

"They stood
before the king,
and were permitted,
or rather commanded,
that they should answer
the questions which he
should ask them."
(Mosiah 7:8).

"And because he said
unto them that Christ was
the God, the Father of all things,
and said that he should take upon
him the image of man, and it should be
the image after which man was created in
the beginning; or in other words, he said
that man was created after the image
of God, and that God should come
down among the children of men,
and take upon him flesh and
blood, and go forth upon
the face of the earth."
(Mosiah 7:27).

"A seer can know
of things which are past,
and also of things which are
to come, and by them shall
all things be revealed, or,
rather, shall secret things
be made manifest, and
hidden things shall
come to light."
(Mosiah 8:17).

"These are they whose
sins he has borne; these are they
for whom he has died, to redeem
them from their transgressions. And
now, are they not his seed? Yea, and
are not the prophets, every one that has
opened his mouth to prophesy, that has not
fallen into transgression, I mean all
the holy prophets ever since the
world began? I say unto you
that they are his seed."
(Mosiah 15:12-13).

"The resurrection of all the prophets, and all those that have believed on their words, or all those that have kept the commandments of God, shall come forth in the first resurrection; therefore, they are the first resurrection." (Mosiah 15:22).

50

"They
carried him upon
the top of the hill Manti,
and there he was caused, or
rather did acknowledge, between
the heavens and the earth, that
what he had taught to the
people was contrary to
the word of God."
(Alma 1:15).

"And thus he cleared the ground, or rather the bank, which was on the west of the river Sidon." (Alma 2:34).

"This he did that he himself might go forth among his people, or among the people of Nephi." (Alma 4:19).

"Whosoever did
belong to the church
that did not repent of
their wickedness and humble
themselves before God — I mean
those who were lifted up in the pride
of their hearts — the same were rejected,
and their names were blotted out."
(Alma 6:3).

"I, Alma, having been commanded of God that I should take Amulek and go forth and preach again unto this people, or the people who were in the city of Ammonihah, it came to pass as I began to preach unto them, they began to contend with me."
(Alma 9:1).

"I never have known much of the ways of the Lord, and his mysteries and marvelous power. I said I never had known much of these things; but behold, I mistake, for I have seen much of his mysteries and his marvelous power; yea, even in the preservation of the lives of this people."
(Alma 10:5)

"When
Amulek had
finished these words
the people began again
to be astonished, and also
Zeezrom began to tremble.
And thus ended the words
of Amulek, or this is all
that I have written."
(Alma 11:46).

This
priesthood being after
the order of his Son, which
order was from the foundation
of the world; or in other words,
being without beginning of days
or end of years, being prepared
from eternity to all eternity,
Now they were ordained
after this manner."
(Alma 13:7-8).

"The Spirit constraineth me
that I must not stretch forth mine
hand; for behold the Lord receiveth them
up unto himself, in glory; and he doth suffer
that they may do this thing, or that the people
may do this thing unto them, according to the
hardness of their hearts, that the judgments
which he shall exercise upon them in his
wrath may be just; and the blood
of the innocent shall stand as
a witness against them, yea,
and cry mightily against
them at the last day."
(Alma 14:11).

"Ammon being the chief among them, or rather he did administer unto them, and he departed from them, after having blessed them according to their several stations, having imparted the word of God unto them, or administered unto them before his departure."
(Alma 17:18).

"As sure as the Lord liveth, so sure as many
as believed, or as many as were brought to the
knowledge of the truth, through the preaching of
Ammon and his brethren, according to the spirit
of revelation and of prophecy, and the power
of God working miracles in them — yea,
I say unto you, as the Lord liveth, as
many of the Lamanites as believed
in their preaching, and were
converted unto the Lord,
never did fall away."
(Alma 23:6).

"And thus we see that they buried their weapons of peace, or they buried their weapons of war, for peace."
(Alma 24:19).

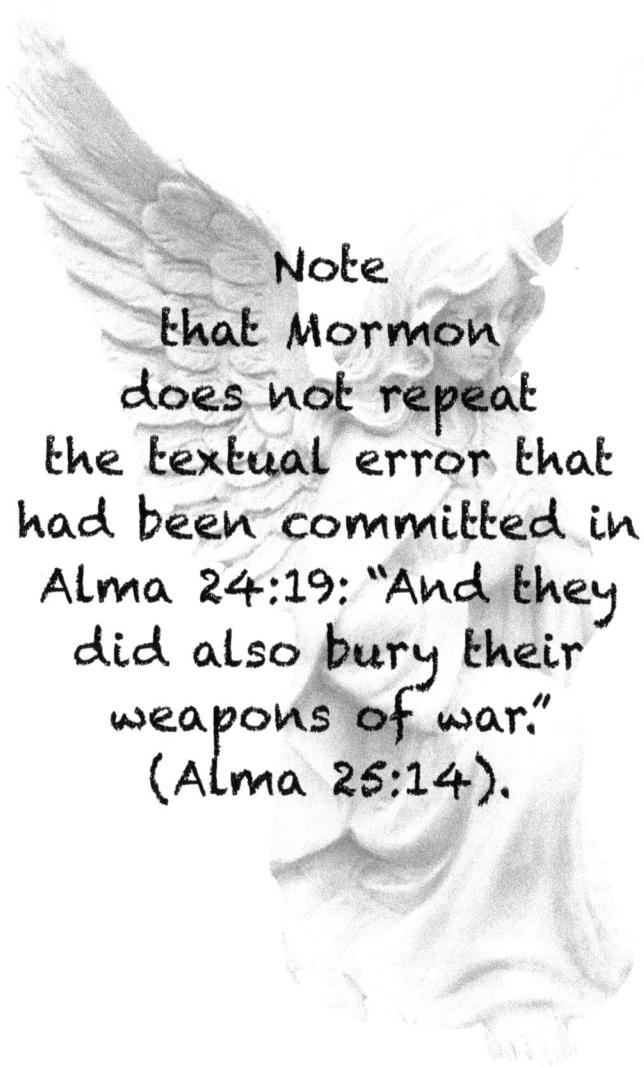

Note
that Mormon
does not repeat
the textual error that
had been committed in
Alma 24:19: "And they
did also bury their
weapons of war."
(Alma 25:14).

"And now behold, we have come, and been forth amongst them; and we have been patient in our sufferings, and we have suffered every privation; yea, we have traveled from house to house, relying upon the mercies of the world — not upon the mercies of the world alone but upon the mercies of God."
(Alma 26:28).

Nor does he
make the error that
was committed in Alma
24:19 in Alma 26:32, when
he again uses the correct
phrase: "They have buried
their weapons of war."
(Alma 26:32).

80

"Now if a
man desired to
serve God, it was his
privilege; or rather, if he
believed in God, it was his
privilege to serve him."
(Alma 30:9).

"Blessed are they who
humble themselves without
being compelled to be humble,
or rather, in other words, blessed is
he that believeth in the word of
God, and is baptized without
stubbornness of heart."
(Alma 32:16).

84

"Now Alma, being
grieved for the iniquity of
his people, yea for the wars, and
the bloodsheds, and the contentions
which were among them; and having
been to declare the word, or sent
to declare the word ... his heart
was exceedingly sorrowful."
(Alma 35:15).

"Yea, I had murdered many of his children, or rather led them away unto destruction." (Alma 36:14).

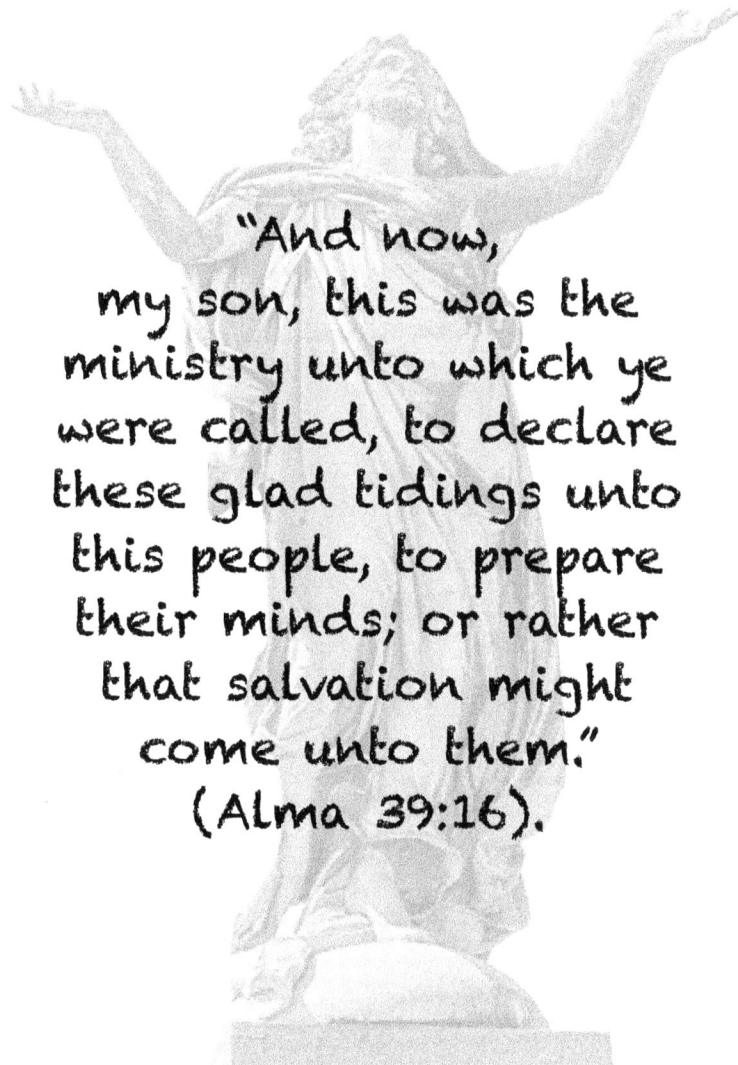

"And now, my son, this was the ministry unto which ye were called, to declare these glad tidings unto this people, to prepare their minds; or rather that salvation might come unto them."
(Alma 39:16).

"I say unto you, that
there is no resurrection — or, I
would say, in other words, that this
mortal does not put on immortality,
this corruption does not put on
incorruption — until after
the coming of Christ."
(Alma 40:2).

"Whether the
souls and the bodies
of those of whom has been
spoken shall all be reunited at
once, the wicked as well as the
righteous, I do not say. Let it
suffice that I say that they all
come forth; or in other words,
their resurrection cometh to
pass before the resurrection
of those who die after the
resurrection of Christ."
(Alma 40:19).

"All men
that are in
a state of nature,
or I would say, in a
carnal state, are in the
gall of bitterness and in
the bonds of iniquity."
(Alma 41:11).

"There was, now and then, a man fell among the Nephites, by their swords and the loss of blood, they being shielded from the more vital parts of the body, or the more vital parts of the body being shielded from the strokes of the Lamanites, by their breastplates, and their arm shields, and their head plates; and thus the Nephites did carry on the work of death among the Lamanites."
(Alma 43:38)

"When Moroni
had proclaimed
these words, behold, the
people came running together
with their armor girded about their
loins, rending their garments in token, or
as a covenant, that they would not forsake
the Lord their God; or, in other words, if they
should transgress the commandments of God,
or fall into transgression, and be ashamed to
take upon them the name of Christ, the Lord
should rend them even as they had
rent their garments."
(Alma 46:21).

"And this was their faith, that by
so doing God would prosper them in
the land, or in other words, if they were
faithful in keeping the commandments of
God that he would prosper them in the
land; yea, warn them to flee, or to
prepare for war, according
to their danger."
(Alma 48:15).

"Behold, the people who were in the land Bountiful, or rather Moroni, feared that they would hearken to the words of Morianton." (Alma 50:32).

"Teancum, by the orders of Moroni, caused that they should commence laboring in digging a ditch round about the land, or the city, Bountiful." (Alma 53:3).

"I have somewhat
to say concerning the people
of Ammon, who, in the beginning
were Lamanites; but by Ammon and
his brethren, or rather by the power
and word of God, they had been
converted unto the Lord."
(Alma 53:10).

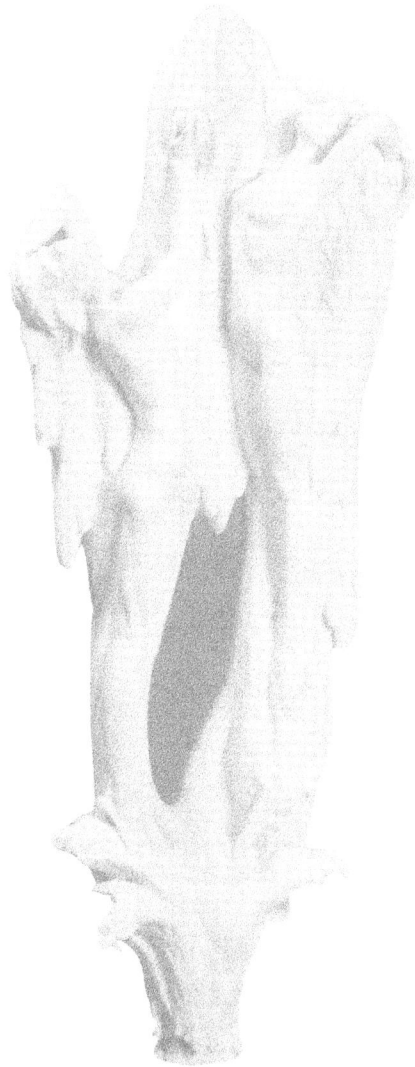

"I have
written unto you
somewhat concerning
this war, which ye have
waged against my people,
or rather which thy brother
hath waged against them."
(Alma 54:5).

"These are the
cities of which the
Lamanites have obtained
possession by the shedding
of the blood of so many of our
valiant men; the land of Manti,
or the city of Manti, and
the city of Zeezrom."
(Alma 56:13-14).

"In the end
of this book ye shall
see that this Gadianton
did prove the overthrow, yea
almost the entire destruction
of the people of Nephi. Behold, I
do not mean the end of the book
of Helaman, but I mean the end of
the book of Nephi, from which I
have taken all the account
which I have written."
(Helaman 2:13-14).

"In the
fifty and first
year of the reign of the
judges there was peace also,
save it were the pride which
began to enter into the church
– not the church of God, but
into the hearts of the people
who professed to belong
to the church of God."
(Helaman 3:33).

"He hath
given unto you that ye might
choose life or death; and ye can do
good and be restored unto that which
is good, or have that which is good
restored unto you; or ye can do
evil, and have that which is
evil restored unto you."
(Helaman 14:30-31).

"I write unto you, desiring
that ye would yield up unto this
my people, your cities, your lands,
and your possessions, rather than that
they should visit you with the sword, and
that destruction should come upon you. Or
in other words, yield yourselves up unto us,
and unite with us and become acquainted
with our secret works, and become our
brethren, that ye may be like unto
us — not our slaves, but our
brethren and partners of
all our substance."
(3 Nephi 3:6-7).

"There
began to be men
inspired from heaven
and sent forth, standing
among the people in all the
land, preaching and testifying
boldly of the sins and iniquities
of the people, and testifying unto them
concerning the redemption which the Lord
would make for his people, or in other
words, the resurrection of Christ;
and they did testify boldly of
his death and sufferings."
(3 Nephi 6:20).

"The
remnant of the seed,
who shall be scattered
forth upon the face of the
earth because of their unbelief,
may be brought in, or may be
brought to a knowledge of
me, their Redeemer."
(3 Nephi 16:4).

"Behold, my joy is
great, even unto fulness,
because of you, and also this
generation; yea, and even the
Father rejoiceth, and also all
the holy angels, because of you
and this generation; for none of
them are lost. Behold, I would
that ye should understand; for
I mean them who are now alive
of this generation; and none
of them are lost; and in
them I have fulness
of joy." (3 Nephi
27:30-31).

"And now, behold, as I
spake concerning those whom the
Lord hath chosen, yea, even three who
were caught up into the heavens, that I
knew not whether they were cleansed from
mortality to immortality – But behold, since I
wrote, I have inquired of the Lord, and he hath
made it manifest unto me that there must
needs be a change wrought upon their
bodies, or else it needs be that
they must taste of death."
(3 Nephi 28:36-37).

128

"Little children cannot (or need not) repent; wherefore, it is awful wickedness to deny the pure mercies of God unto them, for they are all alive in him because of his mercy." (Moroni 8:19).

Afterword

There
is yet another
interesting insight
into the awkwardness
of working with
metal plates.

Mormon knew that
his abridgment of the Book
of Lehi, which ended when King
Benjamin was an old man and ready
to die, would be lost by Sydney Rigdon
during the translation process by Joseph
Smith. Without it, Book of Mormon
readers would not have had
access to the account
of his life.

The Book of Omni, which
is a portion of the Small Plates
of Nephi, deals with King Benjamin
in only three of its verses, and what
Mormon had written about him in the
Book of Mosiah was confined to the
last three years of the king's life.

The Words of Mormon, tacked on
to the end of the Small Plates, serve
as a bridge between the Small Plates and
Mormon's abridgment that follows, beginning
with the Book of Mosiah. Verses 15 - 18 flow
as if Mormon, knowing that there was so
little room left on the Small Plates of
Nephi, hastily finished the record
in uncharacteristically
awkward style.

140

Perhaps the straitened
circumstances under which
he labored help to explain
the fact that one run-on
sentence of 172 words
makes up these
four verses.

"And it came to
pass that after there had been false
Christs, and their mouths had been shut,
and they punished according to their crimes;
And after there had been false prophets, and
false preachers and teachers among the people,
and all these having been punished according
to their crimes; and after there having been
much contention and many dissensions
away unto the Lamanites, behold, it
came to pass that king Benjamin,
with the assistance of the
holy prophets who were
among his people —

144

For
behold,
King Benjamin
was a holy man, and
he did reign over his
people in righteousness;
and there were many holy
men in the land, and they did
speak the word of God with
power and with authority;
and they did use much
sharpness because of
the stiffneckedness
of the people –

Wherefore, with
the help of these, king
Benjamin, by laboring with
all the might of his body and
the faculty of his whole soul, and
also the prophets, did once more
establish peace in the land."
(Words of Mormon
1:15-18).

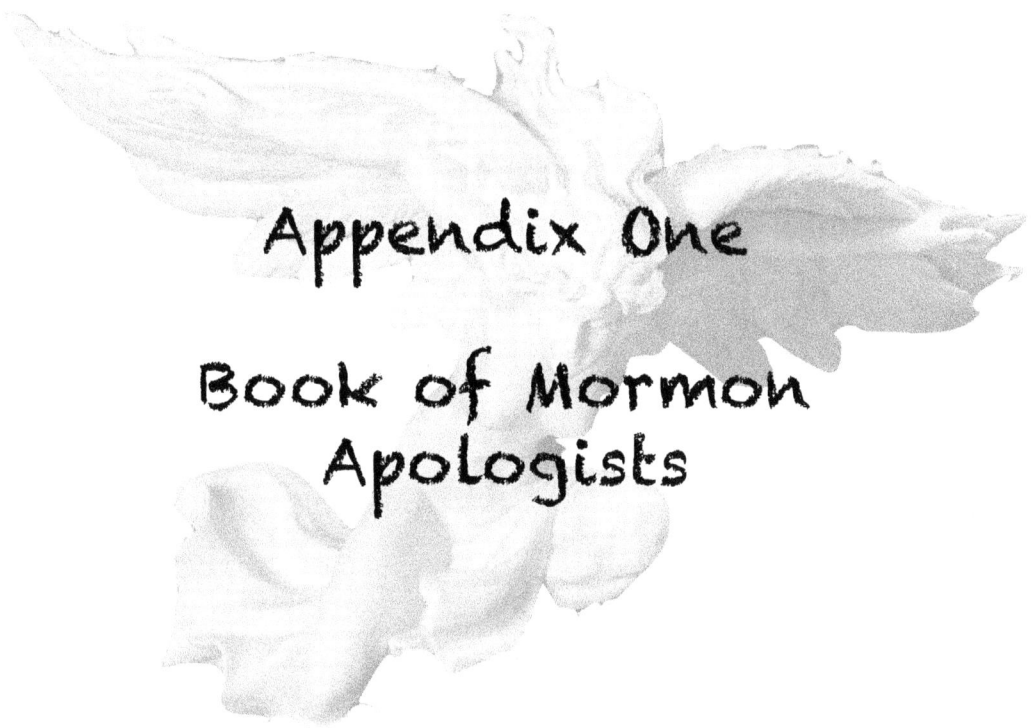

Appendix One

Book of Mormon
Apologists

"Thou
hast made us
that we could write
but little, because of the
awkwardness of our hands."
(Ether 12:24).

152

"When we write we behold our weakness, and stumble because of the placing of our words; and I fear lest the Gentiles shall mock at our words."
(Ether 12:25).

154

"Condemn me
not because of mine
imperfections, neither my
father, neither them who have
written before him; but rather give
thanks unto God that He hath made
manifest unto you our imperfections,
that ye may learn to be more
wise than we have been."
(Mormon 9:31).

Appendix Two

Scripture Citations
in Chronological Order

1 Nephi 1 Superscript

1 Nephi 8:2

1 Nephi 10:4

1 Nephi 14:3

1 Nephi 14:23

1 Nephi 19:6

1 Nephi 19:7

1 Nephi 20:1

2 Nephi 2:5-6

2 Nephi 9:4

2 Nephi 33:8

Jacob 4:1

Jacob 4:4

Jacob 4:18

Words of Mormon 1:15-18

Mosiah 4:6

Mosiah 4:14

Mosiah 4:24

Mosiah 5:2

Mosiah 7:1

Mosiah 7:8

Mosiah 7:27

Mosiah 8:17

Mosiah 15:12-13

Mosiah 15:22

Alma 1:15

Alma 2:34

Alma 4:19

Alma 6:3

Alma 9:1

Alma 10:5

Alma 11:46

Alma 13:7-8

Alma 14:11

Alma 17:18

Alma 23:6

Alma 24:19

Alma 25:14

Alma 26:28

Alma 26:32

Alma 30:9

Alma 32:16

Alma 35:15

Alma 36:14

Alma 39:16

Alma 40:2

Alma 40:19

Alma 41:11

Alma 43:38

Alma 46:21

Alma 48:15

Alma 50:32

Alma 53:3

Alma 53:10

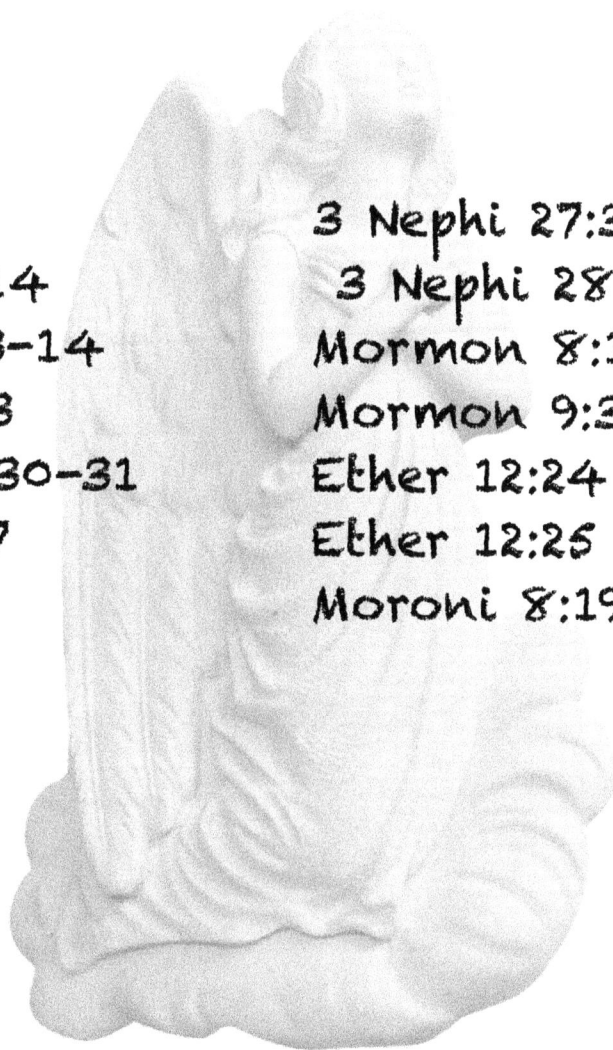

Alma 54:5
Alma 56:13-14
Helaman 2:13-14
Helaman 3:33
Helaman 14:30-31
3 Nephi 3:6-7
3 Nephi 6:20
3 Nephi 16:4

3 Nephi 27:30-31
3 Nephi 28:36-27
Mormon 8:17
Mormon 9:31
Ether 12:24
Ether 12:25
Moroni 8:19

About The Author

Phil Hudson and his wife Jan have 7 children and over 25 grandchildren. They enjoy spending time with their family at their cabin nestled in the Selkirk Mountains, on the shore of Priest Lake, the crown jewel of North Idaho. Phil had a successful dental practice in Spokane, Washington for 43 years, before retiring in 2015. He has an eclectic mix of hobbies, and enjoys the out of doors. He always finds time, however, to record his thoughts on his laptop, and understands Isaac Asimov's response when he was asked: If you knew that you had only 10 minutes left to live, what would you do?" He answered: "I'd type faster."

Phil received the inspiration to write this book while he and Jan were serving as missionaries for The Church of Jesus Christ of Latter-day Saints, in the Kingdom of Tonga. While there, they celebrated their 50th wedding anniversary.

By The Author

Essays

Volume One: Spray From The Ocean Of Thought
Volume Two: Ripples On A Pond
Volume Three: Serendipitous Meanderings
Volume Four: Presents Of Mind
Volume Five: Mental Floss
Volume Six: Fitness Training For The Mind And Spirit

First Principles and Ordinances Series

Faith - Our Hearts Are Changed
Repentance - A Broken Heart and a Contrite Spirit
Baptism - One Hundred And One Reasons Why We Are Baptized
The Holy Ghost - That We Might Have His Spirit To Be With Us
The Sacrament - This Do In Remembrance Of Me

Book of Mormon Commentary

Volume One: Born In The Wilderness
Volume Two: Voices From The Dust
Volume Three: Journey To Cumorah

Doctrine & Covenants Commentary

Volume One - Sections 1 - 34
Volume Two - Sections 35 - 57

Minute Musings: Spontaneous Combustions of Thought

Volume One
Volume Two
Volume Three

Calendars:

As I Think About The Savior
In His Own Words: Discovering William Tyndale
Scriptural Symbols

Children & Youth

Book of Mormon Hiking Song
Happy Birthday
Muddy, Muddy
The Hiawatha Trail: An Allegory
The Little Princess
The Parable of The Pencil
The Thirteen Articles of Faith

Doctrinal Themes

Are Christians Mormon? Volume One
Are Christians Mormon? Volume One
Christmas is The Season When...
Dentistry in The Scriptures
Gratitude
Hebrew Poetry
Hiding in Plain Sight
One Hundred Questions Answered by The Book of Mormon
The Highways and Byways of Life
The House of The Lord
The Parable of The Pencil
Without The Book of Mormon
Writing on Metal Plates

A Thought For Each Day of the Year

Baptism
Faith
Life's Greatest Questions
Repentance
Revelation
The Atonement
The Holy Ghost
The House of the Lord
The Plan of Salvation
The Sabbath
The Sacrament

Professional Publications

Diode Laser Soft Tissue Surgery Volume One
Diode Laser Soft Tissue Surgery Volume Two
Diode Laser Soft Tissue Surgery Volume Three

These, and other titles, are available from online retailers.

Quid magis
possum dicere?

www.ingramcontent.com/pod-product-compliance
Lightning Source LLC
Chambersburg PA
CBHW061757260326
41914CB00006B/1142